LUCY

<small>To</small>

KYLE

<small>From</small>

Words to Warm a Woman's Heart
© 2008 Summerside Press
www.summersidepress.com

Cover & Interior Design by
Müllerhaus Publishing Group | www.mullerhaus.net

Scripture references are from the following sources: The Holy Bible, New International Version® NIV®. © 1973, 1978, 1984 by International Bible Society. Used by permission of Zondervan. The New King James Version (NKJV). Copyright © 1982 by Thomas Nelson, Inc. Used by permission. The Holy Bible, New Living Translation® (NLT). Copyright © 1996, 2004. Used by permission of Tyndale House Publishers, Inc., Wheaton, Illinois. The Message © 1993, 1994, 1995, 1996, 2000, 2001, 2002 by Eugene Peterson. Used by permission of NavPress, Colorado Springs, CO. The New Century Version® (NCV). Copyright © 1987, 1988, 1991 by Thomas Nelson, Inc. Used by permission. All rights reserved.

Excluding Scripture verses, references to men and masculine pronouns have been replaced with gender-neutral references.

ISBN 978-1-934770-40-5

Printed in China

WORDS TO WARM
· · · A · · ·
Woman's
HEART

summerside
PRESS

TABLE OF CONTENTS

The Most Beautiful Things

May God give you eyes to see beauty
only the heart can understand.

Beauty puts a face on God. When we gaze at nature, at a loved one, at a work of art, our soul immediately recognizes and is drawn to the face of God.

MARGARET BROWNLEY

Taking joy in life is a woman's best cosmetic.

ROSALIND RUSSELL

The best and most beautiful things in the world cannot be seen or even touched. They must be felt with the heart.

HELEN KELLER

You are God's created beauty and the focus of His affection and delight.

JANET WEAVER SMITH

Isn't it a wonderful morning? The world looks like
something God had just imagined for His own pleasure.

LUCY MAUD MONTGOMERY

As God's workmanship, we deserve to be treated, and to
treat ourselves, with affection and affirmation, regardless
of our appearance or performance.

MARY ANN MAYO

Just as each day brims with Your beauty,
my mouth brims with praise.

PSALM 71:8 THE MESSAGE

In all ranks of life the human heart
yearns for the beautiful, and the beautiful
things that God makes
are His gift to all alike.

HARRIET BEECHER STOWE

God has a wonderful plan for each person.... He knew
even before He created this world what beauty He would
bring forth from our lives.

Louis B. Wyly

One cannot collect all the beautiful shells on the beach.
One can collect only a few, and they are
more beautiful if they are few.

Anne Morrow Lindbergh

A strong positive mental attitude will create more
miracles than any wonder drug.

Patricia Neal

*I've never seen a smiling face
that was not beautiful.*

Your beauty and love chase after me every day of my life.
I'm back home in the house of God for the rest of my life.

PSALM 23:6 THE MESSAGE

Today a new sun rises for me;
everything lives, everything is animated,
everything seems to speak to me of my passion,
everything invites me to cherish it.

ANNE DE LENCLOS

You should clothe yourselves...with the beauty
that comes from within, the unfading beauty
of a gentle and quiet spirit,
which is so precious to God.

1 Peter 3:4 NLT

Beauty without virtue is a flower without perfume.

Something deep in all of us yearns for God's beauty,
and we can find it no matter where we are.

Sue Monk Kidd

Let there be many windows in your soul,
That all the glory of the universe may beautify it.

Ella Wheeler Wilcox

Blessings Are Extraordinary Gifts

Some blessings—like rainbows after rain or a friend's listening ear—are extraordinary gifts waiting to be discovered in an ordinary day.

Strength, rest, guidance, grace, help, sympathy, love—
all from God to us! What a list of blessings!

EVELYN STENBOCK

Lift up your eyes. Your heavenly Father waits to bless
you—in inconceivable ways to make your life
what you never dreamed it could be.

ANNE ORTLUND

All the way my Saviour leads me—
What have I to ask beside?
Can I doubt His tender mercy,
Who through life has been my guide?
Heavenly peace, divinest comfort,
Here by faith in Him to dwell!
For I know, what'er befall me,
Jesus doeth all things well.

FANNY J. CROSBY

*When You grant a blessing, O Lord,
it is an eternal blessing!*

1 CHRONICLES 17:27 NLT

I will let God's peace infuse every part of today.
As the chaos swirls and life's demands
pull at me on all sides, I will breathe in
God's peace that surpasses all understanding.
He has promised that He would set within me
a peace too deeply planted to be affected by
unexpected or exhausting demands.

Let God's promises shine on your problems.

CORRIE TEN BOOM

May your footsteps set you upon
a lifetime of love.
May you wake each day with His blessings
and sleep each night in His keeping,
and may you always walk
in His tender care

*Add to your joy
by counting your blessings.*

God has not promised sun without rain,
joy without sorrow, peace without pain.
But God has promised strength for the day,
rest for the labor, light for the way,
grace for the trials, help from above,
unfailing sympathy, undying love.

ANNIE JOHNSON FLINT

Blessed is the person who is too busy to worry in the
daytime and too sleepy to worry at night.

CAROLINE SCHROEDER

I wish I had a box,
the biggest I could find,
I'd fill it right up to the brim
with everything that's kind.
A box without a lock, of course,
and never any key;
for everything inside that box
would then be offered free.
Grateful words for joys received
I'd freely give away.
Oh, let us open wide a box
of praise for every day.

How great is Your goodness,
which You have stored up for those who fear You,
which You bestow in the sight of men
on those who take refuge in You.

PSALM 31:19 NIV

15

Tarry at the promise till God meets you there.
He always returns by way of His promises.

L. B. COWMAN

I will bless you and make your name great,
and you will be a blessing.

GENESIS 12:2 NIV

We don't have to be perfect to be a blessing.
We are asked only to be real, trusting
in His perfection to cover our imperfection,
knowing that one day we will finally be
all that Christ saved us for
and wants us to be.

GIGI GRAHAM TCHIVIDJIAN

Sweet
Contentment

Love, consolation and peace bloom only
in the garden of sweet contentment.

Martha Anderson

Women of adventure have conquered their fates
and know how to live exciting and fulfilling lives
right where they are. They have learned to
reinvent themselves and find creative ways
to enjoy the world and their place in it.
They know how to take mini-vacations,
stop and smell the roses,
and live fully in the moment.

BARBARA JENKINS

Contentment is not the fulfillment of what you want,
but the realization of how much you already have.

You're blessed when you're content with just who you
are—no more, no less. That's the moment you find
yourselves proud owners of everything that can't
be bought.

MATTHEW 5:5 THE MESSAGE

It is always wise to stop wishing for things long enough to
enjoy the fragrance of those now flowering.

PATRICE GIFFORD

An unhurried sense of time is in itself
a form of wealth.

BONNIE FRIEDMAN

Where the soul is full of peace and joy,
outward surroundings and circumstances
are of comparatively little account.

HANNAH WHITALL SMITH

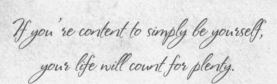

If you're content to simply be yourself,
your life will count for plenty.

MATTHEW 23:11 THE MESSAGE

Let the day suffice, with all its joys and failings,
its little triumphs and defeats. I'd happily,
if sleepily, welcome evening as a time of rest,
and let it slip away, losing nothing.

KATHLEEN NORRIS

I am still determined to be cheerful and happy,
in whatever situation I may be;
for I have also learned from experience
that the greater part of our happiness or misery
depends upon our dispositions,
and not upon our circumstances.

MARTHA WASHINGTON

Our fulfillment comes in knowing God's glory,
loving Him for it, and delighting in it.

For I have learned in whatever state I am, to be content.
I know what it is to be in need, and I know what it is to
have plenty. I have learned the secret of being content
in any and every situation, whether well fed or hungry,
whether living in plenty or in want.

PHILIPPIANS 4:11-12 NKJV

Life is not intended to be simply a round
of work, no matter how interesting and important
that work may be. A moment's pause to watch
the glory of a sunrise or a sunset is soul satisfying,
while a bird's song will set the steps
to music all day long.

LAURA INGALLS WILDER

Normal day, let me be aware of the
treasure you are. Let me learn from you,
love you, bless you before you depart.
Let me not pass you by in quest
of some rare and perfect tomorrow.

The splendor of the rose and the whiteness of
the lily do not rob the little violet of its scent
nor the daisy of its simple charm.
If every tiny flower wanted to be a rose,
spring would lose its loveliness.

THÉRÈSE OF LISIEUX

To love is to be content with the present moment, open to
its meaning, entering into its mystery.

ELIZABETH O'CONNOR

Happy times and bygone days are never lost....
In truth, they grow more wonderful
within the heart that keeps them.

KAY ANDREW

Encouragement for Your Heart

The Scriptures give us hope and encouragement as we
wait patiently for God's promises to be fulfilled.

ROMANS 15:4 NLT

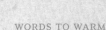
God created us with an overwhelming desire to soar.
Our desire to develop and use every ounce of
potential He's placed in us is not egotistical.
He designed us to be tremendously productive
and "to mount up with wings like eagles,"
realistically dreaming of what
He can do with our potential.

CAROL KENT

God makes our lives a medley of joy and tears,
hope and help, love and encouragement.

I wanted you to see what real courage is…. It's when you
know you're licked before you begin but you begin
anyway and you see it through no matter what.

HARPER LEE

Moments spent listening, talking, playing, and sharing
together may be the most important times of all.

GLORIA GAITHER

Hope begins in the dark, the stubborn hope that if you
just show up and try to do the right thing, the dawn will
come. You wait and watch and work: You don't give up.

ANNE LAMOTT

For we have great joy and consolation
in your love, because the hearts of the saints
have been refreshed by you.

PHILEMON 1:7 NKJV

So when some dear joy loses
its beauteous summer glow,
Think how the roots of roses
are kept alive in the snow.

ALICE CARY

When we take time to notice the simple things in life,
we never lack for encouragement.
We discover we are surrounded by a limitless hope
that's just wearing everyday clothes.

May our Lord Jesus Christ Himself and God
our Father encourage you and strengthen you
in every good thing you do and say.

2 Thessalonians 2:16 ncv

Every day we live is a priceless gift of God,
loaded with possibilities to learn something new,
to gain fresh insights.

Dale Evans Rogers

Encouragement is being a good listener,
being positive, letting others know you accept them
for who they are. It is offering hope,
caring about the feelings of another, understanding.

Gigi Graham Tchividjian

We are so preciously loved by God that we cannot even
comprehend it. No created being can ever know how
much and how sweetly and tenderly God loves them.

Julian of Norwich

A word of encouragement to those we meet,
a cheerful smile in the supermarket, a card or letter to a
friend, a readiness to witness when opportunity is given—
all are practical ways in which we may let His light shine
through us.

ELIZABETH B. JONES

*There are times when encouragement means
such a lot. And a word is enough to convey it.*

GRACE STRICKER DAWSON

Calm me, O Lord, as You stilled the storm,
Still me, O Lord, keep me from harm.
Let all the tumult within me cease,
Enfold me, Lord, in Your peace.

CELTIC TRADITIONAL

Some days, it is enough encouragement just to watch
the clouds break up and disappear, leaving behind
a blue patch of sky and bright sunshine that is
so warm upon my face. It's a glimpse of divinity;
a kiss from heaven.

The stars exist that we might know
how high our dreams can soar.

Everyone has inside himself a piece of good news!
The good news is that you really don't know
how great you can be, how much you can love,
what you can accomplish and
what your potential is.

ANNE FRANK

A Treasury
of Faith

In the end, I think this is what women truly desire:
to know God and to stand tall in their faith,
strong at the core, tender in heart.

RUTH SENTER

Faith means being sure of what we hope for...now.
It means knowing something is real, this moment,
all around you, even when you don't see it.
Great faith isn't the ability to believe
long and far into the misty future.
It's simply taking God at His word
and taking the next step.

JONI EARECKSON TADA

Now faith is the substance of things hoped for,
the evidence of things not seen.

HEBREWS 11:1 NCV

The soft, sweet summer was warm and glowing,
Bright were the blossoms on every bough:
I trusted Him when the roses were blooming;
I trust Him now....

L. B. COWMAN

You are a child of your heavenly Father.
Confide in Him. Your faith in His love and power
can never be bold enough.

BASILEA SCHLINK

*Only she who can see the invisible
can do the impossible.*

The Lord your God is indeed God.
He is the faithful God who keeps His covenant
for a thousand generations and lavishes
His unfailing love on those who love Him
and obey His commands.

DEUTERONOMY 7:9 NLT

Faith sees the invisible, believes the incredible,
and receives the impossible.

I believe in the sun even if it isn't shining.
I believe in love even when I am alone.
I believe in God even when He is silent.

Faith is the first factor in a life devoted to service.
Without faith, nothing is possible.
With it, nothing is impossible.
MARY MCLEOD BETHUNE

If it can be verified, we don't need faith....
Faith is for that which lies on the other side of reason.
Faith is what makes life bearable, with all its
tragedies and ambiguities and sudden, startling joys.
MADELEINE L'ENGLE

*Faith expects from God what is
beyond all expectations.*

Within each of us there is an inner place
where the living God Himself longs to dwell,
our sacred center of belief.

There is no unbelief;
Whoever plants a seed beneath the sod
And waits to see it push away the clod,
She trusts in God.

ELIZABETH YORK CASE

Faith is not an effort, a striving, a ceaseless seeking,
as so many earnest souls suppose, but rather a letting go,
an abandonment, an abiding rest in God that nothing,
not even the soul's shortcomings, can disturb.

I think miracles exist in part as gifts and in part as clues
that there is something beyond the flat world we see.

PEGGY NOONAN

I took an inventory and looked into my little bag to see
what I had left over. I had one jewel left in the bag,
the brightest jewel of all. I had the gift of faith.

LOLA FALANA

Let love and faithfulness never leave you;
bind them around your neck,
write them on the tablet of your heart.

Proverbs 3:3 NIV

Faith has to be exercised in the midst of ordinary,
down-to-earth living.

Elisabeth Elliot

I see Heaven's glories shine,
And faith shines equal, arming me from fear.

Emily Brontë

There is an activity of the spirit, silent, unseen, which
must be the dynamic of any form of truly creative,
fruitful trust. When we commit a predicament,
a possibility, a person to God in genuine confidence,
we do not merely step aside and tap our foot until God
comes through. We remain involved. We remain in
contact with God in gratitude and praise. But we do this
without anxiety, without worry.

Eugenia Price

The Love
of Family

Family faces are magic mirrors.
Looking at people who belong to us,
we see the past, present, and future.

Gail Lumet Buckley

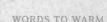
Home. A place where when you get there, you know your
heart has been there all along.

GLORIA GAITHER

Sooner or later we all discover that the important
moments in life are not the advertised ones,
not the birthdays, the graduations, the weddings,
not the great goals achieved.
The real milestones are less prepossessing.
They come to the door of memory.

SUSAN B. ANTHONY

Please, bless my family. Let it continue before You always.
Lord God, You have said so.

2 SAMUEL 7:29 NVC

I feel from a spiritual standpoint that there's a real
celebration of humanity, of the common bond
of everybody. We need each other.

AMY GRANT

We really need only five things on this earth:
Some food, some sun, some work, some fun,
and someone.

BEATRICE NOLAN

Love allows us to live,
and through living we grow in loving.

EVELYN MANDEL

The effect of having other interests beyond
those domestic works well. The more one does
and sees and feels, the more one is able to do,
and the more genuine may be one's appreciation
of fundamental things like home, and love,
and understanding companionship.

AMELIA EARHART

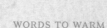

As if that weren't enough, You've blessed my family so that it will continue in Your presence always. Because You have blessed it, God, it's really blessed—blessed for good!

1 CHRONICLES 17:16 THE MESSAGE

We were a strange little band of characters, trudging through life sharing diseases and toothpaste, coveting one another's desserts, hiding shampoo, borrowing money, locking each other out of our rooms, inflicting pain and kissing to heal it in the same instant, loving, laughing, defending, and trying to figure out the common thread that bound us all together.

ERMA BOMBECK

Families give us many things—love and meaning, purpose and an opportunity to give, and a sense of humor.

When you look at your life, the greatest happinesses
are family happinesses.

JOYCE BROTHERS

*We are so very rich if we know just a few
people in a way in which we know no others.*

CATHERINE BRAMWELL-BOOTH

What families have in common the world around
is that they are the place where people learn
who they are and how to be that way.

JEAN ILLSLEY CLARKE

Finally, all of you should be in agreement,
understanding each other, loving each other as family,
being kind and humble.

1 PETER 3:8 NCV

Our job is not to straighten each other out,
but to help each other up.

NEVA COYLE

More and more I realize that everybody,
regardless of age, needs to be hugged and comforted
in a brotherly or sisterly way now and then.
Preferably now.

JANE HOWARD

Family is of the utmost importance to me. But my family
is no more perfect than [any other].... We love, trust, get
hurt, sometimes outraged, and we love and trust anyhow,
because that's the best way to let our love grow.

MADELEINE L'ENGLE

The greatest gift we can give one another is
rapt attention to one another's existence.

SUE ATCHLEY EBAUGH

Nothing Like a True Friend

Insomuch as any one pushes you nearer to God,
he or she is your friend.

FRENCH PROVERB

I cannot count the number of times I have been
strengthened by another woman's heartfelt hug,
appreciative note, surprise gift, or caring questions...
my friends are an oasis to me, encouraging me to go on.
They are essential to my well-being.

DEE BRESTIN

Knowing what to say is not always necessary;
just the presence of a caring friend
can make a world of difference.

SHERI CURRY

What shall I bestow upon a friend?
Gay laughter to sustain when sorrow may bring pain,
a bright song of life, a belief that winter ends
in the glory of spring, and a prayer of hope
for peace that will forever stay.

LEA PALMER

A friend understands what you are trying to say...even
when your thoughts aren't fitting into words.

ANN D. PARRISH

Rich is the woman who has a praying friend.

JANICE HUGHES

Friendship is the fruit gathered from the trees
planted in the rich soil of love,
and nurtured with tender care and understanding.

ALMA L. WEIXELBAUM

Perfume and incense bring joy to the heart,
and the pleasantness of one's friend
springs from his earnest counsel.

PROVERBS 27:9 NIV

The happiest business in all the world
is that of making friends,
And no investment on the street
pays larger dividends,
For life is more than stocks and bonds,
and love than rate percent,
And she who gives in friendship's name
shall reap what she has spent.

Thank you for the treasure
of your friendship...for showing me
God's special heart of love.

A friend hears the song in my heart
and sings it to me when my memory fails.

Reliable friends who do what they say
are like cool drinks in sweltering heat—refreshing!
PROVERBS 25:13 THE MESSAGE

If we would build on a sure foundation in friendship,
we must love friends for their sake
rather than for our own.

CHARLOTTE BRONTË

When you are truly joined in spirit,
another woman's good is your good too.
Your work for the good of each other.

RUTH SENTER

Don't walk in front of me—I may not follow.
Don't walk behind me—I may not lead.
Walk beside me—And just be my friend.

There are some friends you know you will have for the
rest of your life. You're welded together by love, trust,
respect or loss—or simple embarrassment.

Having someone who understands is a great blessing
for ourselves. Being someone who understands
is a great blessing to others.

JANETTE OKE

We should all have one person who knows
how to bless us despite the evidence.

PHYLLIS THEROUX

I am only as strong as the coffee I drink,
the hairspray I use, and the friends I have.

This is My commandment, that you love one other
as I have loved you. Greater love has no one than this,
than to lay down one's life for his friends.

JOHN 15:12-13 NKJV

A true friend is one who is concerned about what we are
becoming, who sees beyond the present relationship and
cares deeply about us as a whole person.

GLORIA GAITHER

You Got a Gift

There's a special kind of freedom women enjoy: freedom to share innermost thoughts, to ask a favor, to show their true feelings. The freedom simply to be themselves.

As women, we want to know we are important
and that we have a significant place in our world.
We need to know that we matter to someone,
that our lives are making a difference
in the lives of other people,
that we are able to touch their souls.
This desire to have value is God-given.

BEVERLY LaHAYE

*If your lips can speak a word of encourage-
ment to a weary soul, you have a talent.*

EVA J. CUMMINGS

Each one of us is God's special work of art. Through us,
He teaches and inspires, delights and encourages,
informs and uplifts all those who view our lives.

JONI EARECKSON TADA

And I have filled him with the Spirit of God, with skill,
ability and knowledge in all kinds of crafts.

EXODUS 31:3 NIV

When I stand before God at the end of my life,
I would hope that I would not have a single bit
of talent left and could say,
"I used everything You gave me."

ERMA BOMBECK

This is the real gift: you have been given
the breath of life, designed with a unique,
one-of-a-kind soul that exists forever—
the way that you choose to live it
doesn't change the fact that you've been given
the gift of being now and forever.
Priceless in value, you are handcrafted by God,
who has a personal design and plan for each of us.

No one can arrive from being talented alone.
God gives talent,
work transforms talent into genius.

ANNA PAVLOVA

We all have different gifts, each of which came
because of the grace God gave us.... Anyone
who has the gift of serving should serve.
Anyone who has the gift of teaching should teach.
Whoever has the gift of encouraging others
should encourage. Whoever has the gift of giving
to others should give freely. Anyone who
has the gift of being a leader should try hard
when he leads. Whoever has the gift of
showing mercy to others should do so with joy.

ROMANS 12:6-8 NCV

God does not ask your ability or your inability.
He asks only your availability.

MARY KAY ASH

Every one has a gift for something,
even if it is the gift of being a good friend.

MARIAN ANDERSON

*Since you are like no other being
ever created since the beginning of time,
you are incomparable.*

BRENDA UELAND

God gave me my gifts. I will do all I can
to show Him how grateful I am to Him.

GRACE LIVINGSTON HILL

Giving encouragement to others is a most welcome gift,
for the results of it are lifted spirits,
increased self-worth, and a hopeful future.

FLORENCE LITTAUER

Lord...give me the gift of faith to be renewed and shared
with others each day. Teach me to live this moment only,
looking neither to the past with regret,
nor the future with apprehension.
Let love be my aim and my life a prayer.

ROSEANN ALEXANDER-ISHAM

God's designs regarding you, and His methods of bringing
about these designs, are infinitely wise.

MADAME JEANNE GUYON

It is clear to us, friends, that God not only loves you
very much but also has put His hand on you
for something special.

1 THESSALONIANS 1:4 THE MESSAGE

God
Our Father

I need not lack now any more
For any lovely thing;
I need to know my birthright for
My Father is the King!

Evelyn Gage

Tuck [this] thought into your heart today.
Treasure it. Your Father God cares about
your daily everythings that concern you.

KAY ARTHUR

Whoever walks toward God one step,
God runs toward him two.

JEWISH PROVERB

God is every moment totally aware of each one of us.
Totally aware in intense concentration and love....
No one passes through any area of life, happy or tragic,
without the attention of God.

EUGENIA PRICE

As a rose fills a room with its fragrance,
so will God's love fill our lives.

MARGARET BROWNLEY

We continually recall before God our Father
the things you have done because of your faith
and the work you have done because of your love.

1 Thessalonians 1:3 ncv

Before anything else, above all else, beyond everything
else, God loves us. God loves us extravagantly,
ridiculously, without limit or condition. God is in love
with us...God yearns for us.

Roberta Bondi

God is the sunshine that warms us,
the rain that melts the frost and waters the young plants.
The presence of God is a climate of strong
and bracing love, always there.

Joan Arnold

The treasure our heart searches for
is found in the ocean of God's love.

Janet Weaver Smith

Nothing we can do will make the Father love us less;
nothing we do can make Him love us more.
He loves us unconditionally with an everlasting love.
All He asks of us is that we respond to Him
with the free will that He has given to us.

NANCIE CARMICHAEL

God is the Father who is full of mercy and all comfort.
He comforts us every time we have trouble,
so when others have trouble, we can comfort them
with the same comfort God gives us.

2 CORINTHIANS 1:3-4 NCV

The Creator thinks enough of you to have sent Someone
very special so that you might have life—abundantly,
joyfully, completely, and victoriously.

*God will never let you be shaken or moved
from your place near His heart.*

JONI EARECKSON TADA

We do not need to search for heaven,
over here or over there, in order to find our eternal Father.
In fact, we do not even need to speak out loud,
for though we speak in the smallest whisper or the most
fleeting thought, He is close enough to hear us.

TERESA OF AVILA

The God who created, names, and numbers the stars
in the heavens also numbers the hairs of my head....
He pays attention to very big things
and to very small ones. What matters to me
matters to Him, and that changes my life.

ELISABETH ELLIOT

People who don't know God and the way He works
fuss over these things, but you know both God
and how He works. Steep yourself in God-reality,
God-initiative, God-provisions. You'll find
all your everyday human concerns will be met.
Don't be afraid of missing out. You're My dearest friends!
The Father wants to give you the very kingdom itself.

LUKE 12:30-32 THE MESSAGE

Stand outside this evening. Look at the stars.
Know that you are special and loved
by the One who created them.

You have the joy of this assurance—the Heavenly Father
will always answer prayer,
and He knows—just how much you can bear.

PHYLLIS HALL

A Heart
Full of
Gratitude

Happiness is a healthy mental attitude, a grateful spirit,
a clear heart full of love.

If it is God who gives prayer, then God often gives it in
the form of gratitude, and gratitude itself, when it is
received attentively in prayer, is healing to the heart.
Prayer is such a mysterious business for something
so ordinary and everyday.

ROBERTA BONDI

That I am here is a wonderful mystery
to which I will respond with joy.

Enter into His gates with thanksgiving,
and into His courts with praise.
Be thankful to Him, and bless His name.

PSALM 100:4 NKJV

Most of the people I know who have what I want—
which is to say, purpose, heart, balance, gratitude, joy—
are people with a deep sense of spirituality....
They are part of something beautiful.

ANNE LAMOTT

*Appreciation is like salt—a little
goes a long way to bring out the best in us.*

Gratitude unlocks the fullness of life. It turns what we
have into enough, and more.... It can turn a meal into a
feast, a house into a home, a stranger into a friend.
Gratitude makes sense of our past, brings peace for today,
and creates a vision for tomorrow.

MELODY BEATTIE

True gratitude, like true love,
must find expression in acts, not words.

R. MILDRED BARKER

Were there no God we would be
in this glorious world with grateful hearts
and no one to thank.

CHRISTINA ROSSETTI

Feeling grateful or appreciative of someone
or something in your life actually attracts more
of the things that you appreciate and value into your life.
And, the more of your life that you like and appreciate,
the healthier you'll be.

CHRISTIANE NORTHRUP

Give thanks to the Lord, for He is good!
His faithful love endures forever.

1 CHRONICLES 16:34 NLT

I am convinced that God has built into all of us an
appreciation of beauty and has even allowed us to
participate in the creation of beautiful things and places.
It may be one way God brings healing to our brokenness,
and a way that we can contribute toward bringing
wholeness to our fallen world.

MARY JANE WORDEN

To receive a gift, molded from love and sacrifice, selected
with care and tied up with all the excitement the giver has
to offer, is indeed rare. They don't come along often,
but when they do, cherish them.

ERMA BOMBECK

Give thanks to God.
Call out His name. Ask Him anything!
Shout to the nations, tell them what He's done,
spread the news of His great reputation!

ISAIAH 12:4 THE MESSAGE

Let us begin from this moment
to acknowledge Him in all our ways,
and do everything, whatsoever we do,
as service to Him and for His glory,
depending upon Him alone for wisdom,
and strength, and sweetness, and patience.

HANNAH WHITALL SMITH

Being grateful for what we have today doesn't mean we
have to have that forever. It means we acknowledge that
what we have today is what we're supposed to have today.
There is enough.... And all we need will come to us.

MELODY BEATTIE

Influence:
the Seasoning
of Life

The blossom cannot tell what becomes of its
fragrance as it drifts away, just as no person can tell
what becomes of her influence as she continues through life.

What a God! His road stretches straight and smooth.
Every God-direction is road-tested.
Everyone who runs toward Him
Makes it.

PSALM 18:30 THE MESSAGE

*Some people make the world special
just by being in it.*

I remember the times you were there for me, showing
real interest and concern. I'm thankful for the closeness
we share. How I enjoy being with you!

The fullness of our heart is expressed in our eyes, in our
touch, in what we write, in what we say, in the way we
walk, the way we receive, the way we need.

MOTHER TERESA

Next to God we are indebted to women, first for life itself,
and then for making it worth living.

MARY MCLEOD BETHUNE

This I learned from the shadow of a tree,
That to and fro did sway against a wall,
Our shadow selves, our influence, may fall
Where we ourselves can never be.

ANNA HAMILTON

I want just one thing. To live long enough to pay back in
some way your undeserved and overwhelming generosity.

PAM BROWN

Where there is no word from God,
people are uncontrolled, but those who obey
what they have been taught are happy.

PROVERBS 29:18 NCV

What we feel, think, and do this moment
influences both our present and the future
in ways we may never know.
Begin. Start right where you are.
Consider your possibilities and find
inspiration... to add more meaning
and zest to your life.

ALEXANDRA STODDARD

Kind words are jewels that live in the heart and soul
and remain as blessed memories
years after they have been spoken.

MARVEA JOHNSON

Many women...have buoyed me up in times of weariness
and stress. Each friend was important.... Their words
have seasoned my life. Influence, just like salt shaken out,
is hard to see, but its flavor is hard to miss.

PAM FARREL

The real secret of happiness
is not what you give or what you receive,
it's what you share.

Now...we ask you to appreciate those who work hard
among you, who lead you in the Lord and teach you.
Respect them with a very special love because of the work
they do. Live in peace with each other.

1 THESSALONIANS 5:12 NCV

Kindness is the only service that will stand the storm
of life and not wash out. It will wear well and be
remembered long after the prism of politeness or the
complexion of courtesy has faded away.

69

Let every woman become so cultivated and
refined in intellect, that her taste and judgement
will be respected...so unassuming and unambitious,
that collision and competition will be banished...then,
the fathers, the husbands, and the sons,
will find an influence thrown around them,
to which they will yield not only willingly but proudly.

<small>Catherine Beecher</small>

There are two kinds of people in the world:
those who come into a room and say,
"Here I am!"
and those who come in and say,
"Ah, there you are!"

Finding Joy

All who seek the Lord will praise Him.
Their hearts will rejoice with everlasting joy.

PSALM 22:26 NLT

*Taking joy in life
is a woman's best cosmetic.*

ROSALIND RUSSELL

How necessary it is to cultivate a spirit of joy.
It is a psychological truth that the physical acts
of reverence and devotion make one feel devout.
The courteous gesture increases one's respect for others.
To act lovingly is to begin to feel loving,
and certainly to act joyfully brings joy to others
which in turn makes one feel joyful.
I believe we are called to the duty of delight.

DOROTHY DAY

I pray that the God who gives hope will fill you with much
joy and peace while you trust in Him. Then your hope will
overflow by the power of the Holy Spirit.

ROMANS 15:13 NCV

To be able to find joy in another's joy,
that is the secret
of happiness.

Where does constant joy abound?
In the restless social round,
Entertainment in excess,
Worldly charm or cleverness?
Fleeting are their seeming gains.
Joy is found where Jesus reigns.

HALLIE SMITH BIXBY

As we grow in our capacities to see and enjoy the joys
that God has placed in our lives, life becomes a glorious
experience of discovering His endless wonders.

God makes our lives a medley of joy and tears,
hope and help, love and encouragement.

Our hearts were made for joy.
Our hearts were made to enjoy the One
who created them. Too deeply planted
to be much affected by the ups and downs of life,
this joy is a knowing and a being known by our Creator.
He sets our hearts alight with radiant joy.

A joyful heart is like a sunshine of God's love,
the hope of eternal happiness, a burning flame of God....
And if we pray, we will become that sunshine
of God's love—in our own home, the place where we live,
and in the world at large.

MOTHER TERESA

Happiness comes of the capacity to feel deeply,
to enjoy simply, to think freely,
to risk life, to be needed.

STORM JAMESON

When hands reach out in friendship,
hearts are touched with joy.

If one is joyful, it means that one is faithfully
living for God, and that nothing else counts;
and if one gives joy to others one is doing God's work.
With joy without and joy within, all is well.

JANET ERSKINE STUART

You have to *look* for the joy.
Look for the light of God that is hitting your life,
and you will find sparkles you didn't know were there.

BARBARA JOHNSON

Happiness is something that comes into our lives through
doors we don't even remember leaving open.

Rose Wilder Lane

Remember: Each of us can decrease
the suffering of the world
by adding to its joy.

Dawna Markova

The Lord is my strength and my shield;
my heart trusts in Him, and I am helped.
My heart leaps for joy
and I will give thanks to Him in song.

Psalm 28:7 niv

Laughter Is a Mini Vacation

Take time to laugh.
It is the music of the soul.

What a circus we women perform every day of our lives.
It puts a trapeze artist to shame.
ANNE MORROW LINDBERGH

Our mouths were filled with laughter,
our tongues with songs of joy.

PSALM 126:2 NIV

Laughing at ourselves
as well as with each other
gives a surprising sense of togetherness.
HAZEL C. LEE

Confidence is the feeling you have before
you understand the situation.

The best laughter, the laughter that can heal,
the laughter that has the truest ring, is the laughter
that flowers out of a love for life and its Giver.

MAXINE HANCOCK

This is a test. It is only a test. If this were your actual life,
you would be given better instructions.

MYRNA NEIMS

If you don't have wrinkles, you haven't laughed enough.

PHYLLIS DILLER

Whole-hearted, ready laughter heals, encourages, relaxes
anyone within hearing distance. The laughter that springs
from love makes wide the space around—
gives room for the loved one to enter in.

EUGENIA PRICE

You can't turn back the clock.
But you can wind it up again.

BONNIE PRUDEN

A cheerful look brings joy to the heart;
good news makes for good health.

PROVERBS 15:30 NLT

Sense of humor; God's great gift
causes spirits to uplift,
Helps to make our bodies mend;
lightens burdens; cheers a friend;
Tickles children; elders grin
at this warmth that glows within;
Surely in the great hereafter
heaven must be full of laughter!

Experience is something you don't get
until just after you need it.

People can be divided into three groups:
Those who make things happen,
those who watch things happen,
and those who wonder what happened.

*A good laugh is as good as a
prayer sometimes.*

LUCY MAUD MONTGOMERY

Today's Forecast: Partly rational with
brief periods of coherent thought
giving way to complete apathy by tonight.

SHERRIE WEAVER

Can it be an accident that "stressed"
is "desserts" spelled backwards?

SUSAN MITCHELL

81

An anxious heart weighs a man down,
but a kind word cheers him up.

PROVERBS 12:25 NIV

"I wonder why people say 'Amen' and not 'A women'?"
Bobby questioned. His little friend replied,
"Because they sing hymns and not hers, silly."

Blessed are they who can laugh at themselves,
for they shall never cease to be amused.

If you can learn to laugh in spite of
the circumstances that surround you,
you will enrich others, enrich yourself,
and more than that, you will last!

BARBARA JOHNSON

Love
All Around

Open your hearts to the love God instills....
God loves you tenderly. What He gives you
is not to be kept under lock and key, but to be shared.

MOTHER TERESA

Love is extravagant in the price it is willing to pay,
the time it is willing to give,
the hardships it is willing to endure,
and the strength it is willing to spend.

JONI EARECKSON TADA

Let's practice real love.
This is the only way we'll know
we're living truly, living in God's reality.
It's also the way to shut down debilitating
self-criticism.... For God is greater than
our worried hearts and knows more about us
than we do ourselves. And friends,
once that's taken care of and we're no longer
accusing or condemning ourselves,
we're bold and free before God!

1 JOHN 3:18-21 THE MESSAGE

*Among God's best gifts to us
are the people who love us.*

There is no need to plead that the love of God shall fill our
hearts as though He were unwilling to fill us.... Love is
pressing around us on all sides like air. Cease to resist it
and instantly love takes possession.

AMY CARMICHAEL

Oh, if we did but love others! How easily the least thing,
the shutting of a door gently, the walking softly,
speaking low, not making a noise, or the choice of a seat,
so as to leave the most convenient to others,
might become occasions of its exercise.

MÈRE ANGÉLIQUE ARNAULD

Love...bears all things, believes all things, hopes all things, endures all things. Love never fails.

1 CORINTHIANS 13:4, 7-8 NKJV

Only He who created the wonders
of the world entwines hearts
in an eternal way.

Trying to find yourself within yourself is like peeling the layers off an onion. When you finish you have nothing but a pile of peelings. The only way to find yourself is to go outside of yourself and love another.

RHONDA S. HOGAN

What we have once enjoyed we can never lose.
All that we love deeply becomes a part of us.

HELEN KELLER

Let us love so well our work shall still be sweeter for our
love, and still our love be sweeter for our work.

ELIZABETH BARRETT BROWNING

Love grows from our capacity to give
what is deepest within ourselves
and also receive what is the deepest within
another person. The heart becomes
an ocean strong and deep, launching all on its tide.

You gave me life and showed me Your unfailing love.
My life was preserved by Your care.

JOB 10:12 NLT

Nothing can separate you from His love,
absolutely nothing.... God is enough for time,
and God is enough for eternity.
God is enough!

HANNAH WHITALL SMITH

Today, see if you can stretch your heart
and expand your love so that it touches not only
those to whom you can give it easily,
but also those who need it so much.

DAPHNE ROSE KINGMA

Give Thanks
and
Sing Praise

Let us give all that lies within us...to pure praise,
to pure loving adoration, and to worship
from a grateful heart—a heart that is trained to look up.

Amy Carmichael

*I will give thanks to the Lord
because of His righteousness
and will sing praise to the name
of the Lord Most High.*

PSALM 7:17 NIV

Being grateful for what we have today
doesn't mean we have to have that forever.
It means we acknowledge that what we have today
is what we're supposed to have today.
There is enough.... And all we need will come to us.

Thanksgiving puts power in living, because it
opens the generators of the heart to respond gratefully,
to receive joyfully, and to react creatively.

Thank You, God, for little things
That often come our way,
The things we take for granted
But don't mention when we pray.
The unexpected courtesy,
The thoughtful kindly deed,
A hand reached out to help us
In the time of sudden need.
Oh, make us more aware, dear God,
Of little daily graces
That come to us with sweet surprise
From never-dreamed-of places.

Let's praise His name! He is holy, He is almighty. He is
love. He brings hope, forgiveness, heart cleansing, peace
and power. He is our deliverer and coming King.
Praise His wonderful name!

LUCILLE M. LAW

I will thank You, Lord, among all the people.
I will sing Your praises among the nations.

PSALM 57:9 NLT

Morning has broken like the first morning,
Blackbird has spoken like the first bird....
Praise with elation, praise every morning,
God's re-creation of the new day!

ELEANOR FARJEON

Let us always offer to God our sacrifice of praise,
coming from lips that speak His name.
Do not forget to do good to others,
and share with them, because
such sacrifices please God.

HEBREWS 13:15-16 NCV

*Live today fully, expressing gratitude
for all you have been,
all you are right now,
and all you are becoming.*

MELODY BEATTIE

Our thanksgiving today should include those
things which we take for granted, and we
should continually praise our God, who is
true to His promise, who has provided
and retained the necessities for our living.

BETTY FUHRMAN

Like supernatural effervescence,
praise will sometimes bubble up
from the joy of simply knowing Christ.
Praise like that is...delight. Pure pleasure!
But praise can also be supernatural determination.
A decisive action. Praise like that is...quiet resolve.
Fixed devotion. Strength of spirit.

JONI EARECKSON TADA

May your life become one of glad and unending praise
to the Lord as you journey through this world,
and in the world that is to come!

TERESA OF AVILA

They that trust the Lord find
many things to praise Him for.
Praise follows trust.

LILY MAY GOULD

Investing in Prayer

Allow your dreams a place in your prayers and plans.
God-given dreams can help you move into the future
He is preparing for you.

BARBARA JOHNSON

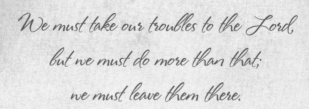

*We must take our troubles to the Lord,
but we must do more than that;
we must leave them there.*

HANNAH WHITALL SMITH

What God gives in answer to our prayers
will always be the thing we most urgently need,
and it will always be sufficient.

ELISABETH ELLIOT

We need quiet time to examine our lives openly and
honestly...spending quiet time alone gives your mind an
opportunity to renew itself and create order.

SUSAN L. TAYLOR

Be kindly affectionate to one another,...
fervent in spirit, serving the Lord;
rejoicing in hope, patient in tribulation,
continuing steadfastly in prayer;
distributing to the needs of the saints,
given to hospitality.

ROMANS 12:10-12 NKJV

There isn't a certain time we should
set aside to talk about God.
God is part of our every waking moment.

MARVA COLLINS

Open wide the windows of our spirits and fill us
full of light; open wide the door of our hearts
that we may receive and entertain Thee
with all the powers of our adoration.

CHRISTINA ROSSETTI

When we call on God,
He bends down His ear to listen,
as a father bends down to listen to his little child.

ELIZABETH CHARLES

Prayer is such an ordinary, everyday,
mundane thing. Certainly, people who
pray are no more saints than the rest of us.
Rather, they are people who want to
share a life with God, to love and be loved,
to speak and to listen, to work
and to be at rest in the presence of God.

ROBERTA BONDI

If a care is too small to be turned into a prayer
then it is too small to be made into a burden.

You pay God a compliment by asking great things of Him

TERESA OF AVILA

The center of power is not to be found in
summit meetings or in peace conferences.
It is not in Peking or Washington or
the United Nations, but rather where a
child of God prays in the power of the Spirit
for God's will to be done in her life,
in her home, and in the world about her.

RUTH BELL GRAHAM

I thank my God every time I remember you. In all my
prayers for all of you, I always pray with joy.

PHILIPPIANS 1:3 NIV

It is when things go wrong,
when good things do not happen,
when our prayers seem to have been lost,
that God is most present.

MADELEINE L'ENGLE

You will make your prayer to Him,
He will hear you.

JOB 22:27 NKJV

Prayer is a long-term investment,
one that will increase your sense of security
because God is your protector.
Keep at it every day, for prayer is
the key of the day and the bolt of the evening.
God is waiting to hear from you.

BARBARA JOHNSON

Priorities
and
Perspectives

Time is a very precious gift of God; so precious that it's
only given to us moment by moment.

<small>AMELIA BARR</small>

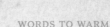

I don't dream of wealth and success for you.
But instead, a job you like, skills you can perfect,
enthusiasms to lighten your heart,
friends, and love in abundance.

PAM BROWN

Let's not get tired of doing what is good....
Therefore, whenever we have the opportunity,
we should do good to everyone.

GALATIANS 6:9-10 NLT

We must know that we have been created for
greater things, not just to be a number in the world,
not just to go for diplomas and degrees....
We have been created in order to love and to be loved.

MOTHER TERESA

We need time to dream, time to remember,
and time to reach the infinite.
Time to be.

GLADYS TABER

Life is about not knowing, having to change,
taking the moment and making the best of it,
without knowing what's going to happen next.
Delicious ambiguity.

GILDA RADNER

Forgetting those things which are behind
and reaching forward to those things which are ahead,
I press toward the goal for the prize
of the upward call of God in Christ Jesus.

PHILIPPIANS 3:13-14 NCV

Blessed is the person who is too busy to worry in the daytime and too sleepy to worry at night.

CAROLINE SCHROEDER

Be still, and in the quiet moments, listen to the voice of your heavenly Father. His words can renew your spirit... no one knows you and your needs like He does.

JANET WEAVER SMITH

Our Lord does not care so much for the importance of our works as for the love with which they are done.

TERESA OF AVILA

We must not, in trying to think about how we can make a big difference, ignore the small daily differences we can make which, over time, add up to big differences that we often cannot foresee.

MARIAN WRIGHT EDELMAN

Make the most of every opportunity.
Be gracious in your speech.
The goal is to bring out the best in others.
COLOSSIANS 4:5 THE MESSAGE

Never let the urgent crowd out the important.

KELLY CATLIN WALKER

Getting things accomplished isn't nearly as important as
taking time for love.
JANETTE OKE

The goal of much that is written about
in life management is to enable us
to do more in less time.
But is this necessarily a desirable goal?
Perhaps we need to get less done,
but the right things.
JEAN FLEMING

Choices can change our lives profoundly.
The choice to mend a broken relationship,
to say yes to a difficult assignment,
to lay aside some important work to play with a child,
to visit some forgotten person—
these small choices may affect our lives eternally.

GLORIA GAITHER

See each morning a world made anew,
as if it were the morning of the very first day;...
treasure and use it, as if it were
the final hour of the very last day.

FAY HARTZELL ARNOLD

Live each day the fullest you can,
not guaranteeing there'll be a tomorrow,
not dwelling endlessly on yesterday.

JANE SEYMOUR

Provisions: a Heavenly Storehouse

Focus your full attention on the goodness and greatness
of your Father rather than on the size of your need.
Your need is so small compared to His ability to meet it.

May you have warm words on a cold evening,
a full moon on a dark night, and the road downhill
all the way to your door.

God's gifts make us truly wealthy.
His loving supply never
shall leave us wanting.

BECKY LAIRD

It is not my business to think about myself.
My business is to think about God.
It is for God to think about me.

SIMONE WEIL

God may not provide us with a perfectly ordered life,
but what He does provide is Himself, His presence,
and open doors that bring us closer to being productive,
positive, and realistic Christian women.

JUDITH BRILES

You know both God and how He works. Steep your life
in God-reality, God-initiative, God-provisions.
Don't worry about missing out. You'll find
all your everyday human concerns will be met.

MATTHEW 6:30 THE MESSAGE

God provides resting places as well as working places.
Rest, then, and be thankful when He brings you,
wearied to a wayside well.

L. B. COWMAN

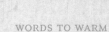

I must simply be thankful, and I am,
for all the Lord has provided for me,
whether big or small in the eyes of someone else.

MABEL P. ADAMSON

A new path lies before us;
We're not sure where it leads;
But God goes on before us,
Providing all our needs.
This path, so new, so different
Exciting as we climb,
Will guide us in His perfect will
Until the end of time.

LINDA MAURICE

God will generously provide all you need.
Then you will always have everything you need
and plenty left over to share with others.

2 CORINTHIANS 9:8 NLT

It is the Lord who provides the sun to light the day
and the moon and stars to light the night, and
who stirs the sea into roaring waves.

JEREMIAH 31:35 NLT

The well of Providence is deep.
It's the buckets we bring to it
that are small.

MARY WEBB

Throughout the Bible, when God asked a man
to do something, methods, means, materials and
specific directions were always provided.
The man had one thing to do: obey.

ELISABETH ELLIOT

You can trust God right now to supply all your needs
for today. And if your needs are more tomorrow,
His supply will be greater also.

There will be days which are great and everything
goes as planned. There will be other days
when we aren't sure why we got out of bed.
Regardless of which kind of day it is, we can be
assured that God takes care of our daily needs.

EMILIE BARNES

Faith is the bucket of power lowered by the rope
of prayer into the well of God's abundance.
What we bring up depends upon what we let down.
We have every encouragement to use a big bucket.

VIRGINIA WHITMAN

Simplicity

It isn't the great big pleasures that count the most;
it's making a great deal out of the little ones.

Jean Webster

Silences make the real conversations
between friends. Not the saying,
but the never needing to say is what counts.

MARGARET LEE RUNBECK

Happy people...enjoy the fundamental,
often very simple things of life....
They savor the moment, glad to be alive,
enjoying their work, their families,
the good things around them.
They are adaptable; they can bend with the wind,
adjust to the changes in their times, enjoy the
contest of life.... Their eyes are turned outward;
they are aware, compassionate.
They have the capacity to love.

JANE CANFIELD

In a world where it is necessary to succeed,
perhaps...we women know more deeply
that success can be a quiet and hidden thing.

PAM BROWN

*Enjoy the little things.
One day you may look back and realize...
they were the big things.*

So in everything, do to others what you would have them
do to you, for this sums up the Law and the Prophets.

MATTHEW 7:12 NIV

While both boredom and serenity
address the passage of time,
the former yawns and rolls its eyes,
the latter sighs and revels in its value.

BARBARA FARMER

It's the little things that make up the richest part of the tapestry of our lives.

A fiery sunset, tiny pansies by the wayside,
the sound of raindrops tapping on the roof—
what extraordinary delight we find in the simple
wonders of life! With wide eyes and full hearts,
we may cherish what others often miss.

A devout life does bring wealth, but it's the rich simplicity
of being yourself before God. Since we entered the world
penniless and will leave it penniless, if we have bread on
the table and shoes on our feet, that's enough.

1 Timothy 6:6 the message

Not every day of our lives is overflowing
with joy and celebration. But there are moments
when our hearts nearly burst within us
for the sheer joy of being alive.
The first sight of our newborn babies,
the warmth of love in another's eyes,
the fresh scent of rain on a hot summer's eve—
moments like these renew in us
a heartfelt appreciation for life.

Gwen Ellis

It is the simple things of life
that make living worthwhile,
the sweet fundamental things such as
love and duty, work and rest,
and living close to nature.

Laura Ingalls Wilder

Don't ever let yourself get so busy that you
miss those little but important extras in life—
the beauty of a day...the smile of a friend...
the serenity of a quiet moment alone.
For it is often life's smallest pleasures and
gentlest joys that make the biggest
and most lasting difference.

The Beauty
of Truth

The simplest and commonest truth seems
new and wonderful when we experience it
the first time in our own life.

Marie von Ebner-Eschenbach

*Truth is always exciting.
Speak it, then.
Life is dull without it.*

PEARL S. BUCK

I am amazed by the sayings of Christ. They seem truer
than anything I have ever read. And they certainly
turn the world upside down.

KATHERINE BUTLER HATHAWAY

Then Jesus said…, "If you abide in My word,
you are My disciples indeed.
And you shall know the truth,
and the truth shall make you free."

JOHN 8:31-32 NKJV

God who is goodness and truth is also beauty.
It is this innate human and divine longing,
found in the company of goodness and truth,
that is able to recognize and leap up at beauty
and rejoice and know that all is beautiful,
that there is not one speck of beauty under the sun
that does not mirror back the beauty of God.

ROBERTA BONDI

It is an extraordinary and beautiful thing that God,
in creation...works with the beauty of matter;
the reality of things; the discoveries of the senses,
all five of them; so that we, in turn,
may hear the grass growing;
see a face springing to life in love and laughter....
The offerings of creation...our glimpses of truth.

MADELIENE L'ENGLE

The wonder of our Lord is that He is so
accessible to us
in the common things of our lives:
the cup of water...breaking of the bread...
welcoming children into our arms...fellowship
over a meal...giving thanks. A simple attitude of
caring, listening, and lovingly telling the truth.

NANCIE CARMICHAEL

Go after a life of love as if your life
depended on it— because it does.
Give yourselves to the gifts God gives you.
Most of all, try to proclaim His truth.

1 CORINTHIANS 14:1 THE MESSAGE

Truth is the only safe ground to stand upon.

ELIZABETH CADY STANTON

Truth is such a rare thing,
it is delightful to tell it.

EMILY DICKINSON

Amid ancient lore the Word of God
stands unique and pre-eminent.
Wonderful in its construction,
admirable in its adaptation,
it contains truths that a child may
comprehend, and mysteries into which
angels desire to look.

FRANCES ELLEN WATKINS HARPER

Every good action and every perfect gift is from God.
These good gifts come down from the Creator
of the sun, moon, and stars, who does not change
like their shifting shadows. God decided to give us
life through the word of truth so we might be
the most important of all the things He made.

JAMES 1:17-18 NCV

Open my eyes that I may see
Glimpses of truth Thou hast for me.
Place in my hands the wonderful key
That shall unclasp and set me free:
Silently now I wait for Thee,
Ready, my God, Thy will to see;
Open my eyes, illumine me, Spirit divine!

CLARA H. SCOTT

A Heart of Wisdom

Teach us to number our days aright,
that we may gain a heart of wisdom.

PSALM 90:12 NIV

A wise gardener plants his seeds,
then has the good sense not to dig them up
every few days to see if a crop is on the way.
Likewise, we must be patient as God brings
the answers...in His own good time.

QUIN SHERRER

*The wise don't expect
to find life worth living;
they make it that way.*

What we need is not new light, but new sight;
not new paths, but new strength to walk in the old ones;
not new duties but new wisdom from on High
to fulfill those that are plain before us.

Oh, how great are God's riches and wisdom and
knowledge! How impossible it is for us to understand
His decisions and His ways!

ROMANS 11:33 NLT

To acquire knowledge, one must study;
but to acquire wisdom, one must observe.

MARILYN VOS SAVANT

We ought to be able to learn things secondhand.
There is not enough time for us
to make all the mistakes ourselves.

HARRIET HALL

At the end of your life you will never regret not having
passed one more test, not winning one more verdict, or
not closing one more deal. You will regret time not spent
with a husband, a friend, a child, or a parent.

BARBARA BUSH

Live your life while you have it. Life is a splendid gift—
there is nothing small about it.

FLORENCE NIGHTINGALE

For the Lord gives wisdom,
and from His mouth come
knowledge and understanding.

PROVERBS 2:6 NIV

I am convinced beyond a shadow of any doubt
that the most valuable pursuit
we can embark upon is to know God.

KAY ARTHUR

Give generously, save consistently, and never spend more
money than you have.

MARY HUNT